Christmas

Fruitcake

Recipes

Laura Sommers is **The Recipe Lady!**

She is a loving wife and mother who lives on a small farm in Baltimore County, Maryland and has a passion for all things domestic especially when it comes to saving money. She has a profitable eBay business and is a couponing addict. Follow her tips and tricks to learn how to make delicious meals on a budget, save money or to learn the latest life hack!

Visit her Amazon Author Page to see her latest books:

amazon.com/author/laurasommers

Visit the Recipe Lady's blog for even more great recipes and to learn which books are **FREE** for download each week:

http://the-recipe-lady.blogspot.com/

Subscribe to The Recipe Lady blog through Amazon and have recipes and updates sent directly to your Kindle:

The Recipe Lady Blog through Amazon

Laura Sommers is also an Extreme Couponer and Penny Hauler! If you would like to find out how to get things for **FREE** with coupons or how to get things for only a **PENNY**, then visit her couponing blog **Penny Items and Freebies**

http://penny-items-and-freebies.blogspot.com/

Other Books by Laura Sommers

- **Christmas Stuffing Recipes**
- **Christmas Hot Chocolate Recipes**
- **Christmas Cookies**
- **Candy Corn Cookbook**
- **Halloween Recipes**
- **50 Pumpkin Recipes**
- **Recipes for Leftover Thanksgiving or Christmas Turkey**

Introduction

Everyone is familiar with Fruitcake. It is the candied sponge cake given at Christmas time as gifts or served after a delicious holiday meal. Sometimes fruitcake is in the shape of a holiday wreath and sometimes it is shaped like a loaf.

But fruitcake has gotten a bad reputation. Mainly because of the unappetizing, mass produced store bought variety. The solution to that is to make your own But there isn't just one recipe out there.

This cookbook is full of mouth-watering delicious Christmas fruitcake recipes for you to try. There are dark varieties, light varieties, regional, rum and whisky filled as well as varieties for the teetotaler among us.

Enjoy one or all of these delicious fruitcake recipes and share with your family and friends.

Traditional Christmas Fruitcake

Ingredients:

1/8 cup chopped dried cherries
1/8 cup chopped dried mango
1/4 cup dried cranberries
1/4 cup dried currants
2 tbsps. chopped candied citron
1/4 cup dark rum 1/2 cup butter
1/4 cup packed brown sugar
1 egg
1/2 cup all-purpose flour
1/8 tsp. baking soda
1/4 tsp. salt
1/4 tsp. ground cinnamon
1/4 cup unsulfured molasses
2 tbsps. milk
1/4 cup chopped pecans
1/4 cup dark rum, divided

Directions:

1. Soak cherries, mango, cranberries, currants, and citron in 1/4 cup rum for at least 24 hours.
2. Cover tightly, and store at room temperature.
3. Preheat oven to 325 degrees F (165 degrees C).
4. Butter a 6x3-inch round pan or loaf pan and line it with parchment paper.
5. In a large bowl, cream together butter and brown sugar until fluffy.
6. Beat in egg.
7. Whisk together flour, baking soda, salt, and cinnamon; mix into butter and sugar in three batches, alternating with molasses and milk.
8. Stir in soaked fruit and chopped nuts. Scrape batter into prepared pan.
9. Bake in preheated oven for 40 to 45 minutes. Cool in the pan for 10 minutes, then sprinkle with 2 tbsps. rum.
10. Cut out one piece parchment paper and one piece cheesecloth, each large enough to wrap around the cake.
11. Moisten cheesecloth with 1 tbsp. rum. Arrange cheesecloth on top of parchment paper, and unmold cake onto it.
12. Sprinkle top and sides of cake with remaining rum.
13. Wrap the cheesecloth closely to the surface of the cake, then wrap with paper.

14. Place in an airtight tin, and age for at least 10 weeks.
15. If storing longer, douse with additional rum for every 10 weeks of storage.

Gumdrop Fruitcake

Ingredients:

1 cup butter
2 cups white sugar
2 eggs, beaten
4 cups all-purpose flour
1 tsp. ground cinnamon
1/4 tsp. ground cloves
1/4 tsp. ground nutmeg
1/4 tsp. salt
1 1/2 cups applesauce
1 tsp. baking soda
1 tbsp. hot water
1 tsp. vanilla extract
16 oz. gumdrops, no black ones
3 cups raisins
1 cup chopped pecans
1 tbsp. butter

Directions:

1. Preheat oven to 325 degrees F (165 degrees C).
2. Line two 9 x 5 inch loaf pans or a 10 inch tube pan with greased parchment or heavy paper.
3. Sift together the flour, cinnamon, cloves, nutmeg, and salt.
4. Cut the gumdrops in fourths. Fry the pecans in the 1 tbsp. butter or margarine.
5. Mix pecans, raisins, and gumdrops together, and roll in 3/4 cup of flour mixture.
6. In a large bowl, cream together 1 cup butter or margarine and white sugar.
7. Mix in beaten eggs.
8. Mix in the flour and spice mixture alternately with the applesauce. Dissolve soda in hot water, and stir into batter.
9. Stir in the vanilla.
10. Stir in nuts, gumdrops, and raisins.
11. Bake for 2 hours. The baking time for the tube pan should be about 30 to 40 minutes longer. Test about 10 minutes before the longer time.
12. You may not get a clean tester, but you will be able to tell if it is the candy gumdrop or dough. Cool.
13. Wrap in foil.

French Fruitcake

Ingredients:

3/4 cup candied orange peel
1/2 cup coarsely chopped walnuts
1/2 cup raisins
1/2 cup golden raisins
2 tbsps. all-purpose flour
1/2 cup butter, softened
1/2 cup white sugar
2 1/2 tbsps. honey
2 eggs
1 1/2 tbsps. light cream
2 tbsps. dark rum
1 tsp. vanilla extract
1 1/2 cups all-purpose flour
1/2 tsp. baking powder

Directions:

1. Toss the candied orange peel, walnuts, and raisins with 2 tbsps. flour. Set aside.
2. In a large bowl, cream the butter with the sugar and honey.
3. Beat in the egg, then the cream or milk, rum, and vanilla.
4. Stir together the remaining 1 1/2 cups flour and the baking powder; beat into the creamed mixture.
5. Stir in the fruits and nuts.
6. Turn the batter into a greased and floured 9 x 5 inch loaf pan.
7. Bake in a preheated 350 degrees F (175 degrees C) oven for 10 minutes. Lower the heat to 325 degrees F (165 degrees C).
8. Bake the cake 45 minutes longer, or until it tests done with a toothpick. Transfer to a rack to cool.

Quick Fruitcake

Ingredients:

2 1/2 cups all-purpose flour, sifted
1 tsp. baking soda
2 eggs, lightly beaten
1 (28 oz.) jar prepared mincemeat pie filling
1 (14 oz.) can sweetened condensed milk
1 cup chopped walnuts
2 cups candied mixed fruit

Directions:

1. Preheat oven to 300 degrees F (150 degrees C).
2. Butter cake pans, and line with wax paper.
3. Butter the wax paper.
4. Sift the flour with the baking soda.
5. In a large bowl, combine eggs, mincemeat, condensed milk, fruit, and nuts.
6. Fold in dry ingredients. Pour into prepared pans.
7. Bake for 2 hours, or until center springs back and top is golden brown.
8. Cool. Turn cakes out onto wire rack; remove wax paper.

Sugarless Fruitcake

Ingredients:

1 cup chopped golden raisins
1/2 tsp. salt
1 1/2 cups chopped walnuts
1 cup chopped cranberries
1 cup unsweetened crushed pineapple
1/4 cup grated lemon peel
1 cup flaked coconut
1/3 cup orange juice
8 packets artificial sweetener
1 tsp. ground mace
1 tsp. ground allspice
1 tsp. baking soda
1 1/2 cups all-purpose flour

Directions:

1. Mix sugar substitute with orange juice. Pour over chopped cranberries.
2. Soak 1 hour, mixing often.
3. Mix raisins, nuts, coconut, lemon rind in flour until well coated.
4. Add cranberries and orange juice mixture.
5. Sprinkle baking soda over mixture, and mix.
6. Mix in spices.
7. Fold in crushed pineapple.
8. Pour batter into a greased and floured 9 inch loaf pan.
9. Bake at 325 degrees F (165 degrees C) for 40 minutes. Cool.

Texas Brazil Nut Fruitcake

Ingredients:

1 cup white sugar
1 pinch salt
1/2 tsp. vanilla extract
4 eggs
1 1/2 cups all-purpose flour
2 tsps. baking powder
1 pound Brazil nuts
1 pound chopped walnuts
1 pound pecan halves
1 pound red candied cherries
1 pound green candied cherries
2 pounds pitted dates

Directions:

1. Preheat oven to 350 degrees F (175 degrees C).
2. Grease three 9x5 inch loaf pans, line them with parchment paper, and grease the paper.
3. Beat eggs, salt and vanilla together until very light and lemon colored.
4. Add sugar, 1 cup of the flour and 2 tsps. baking powder.
5. Put brazil nuts, walnuts, pecans, red and green cherries into a large bowl.
6. Dust with the remaining 1/2 cup flour.
7. Then add the egg and sugar mixture.
8. This is a very stiff mixture.
9. Mix with hands.
10. Press into 3 - 9x5 inch loaf pans which you have lined with parchment paper and have greased both pan and paper.
11. Bake for 1 hour at 350 degrees F (175 degrees C).

New Orleans Fruitcake

Ingredients:

2 cups white sugar
4 eggs
2 tsps. vanilla extract
2 cups all-purpose flour
1 tsp. baking powder
2 pounds pecan halves
1 pound candied cherries
1 pound candied pineapple
1 pound pitted dates

Directions:

1. Preheat oven to 300 degrees F (150 degrees C).
2. Grease and line with parchment paper two 5x9 inch loaf pans.
3. Beat together the eggs, sugar and vanilla until frothy.
4. Sift together the flour and baking powder.
5. Add to the egg mixture.
6. Add the candied cherries, pineapple and dates.
7. Mix well and pour into loaf pans and bake for 1 hour.

Rich Dark Fruitcake

Ingredients:

6 cups sultana raisins
3 cups dried currants
1 1/2 cups pitted dates
6 cups raisins
3 cups candied mixed citrus peel
1/2 pound candied cherries
2 cups almonds
2 cups butter
3 1/4 cups all-purpose flour
3 tsps. baking powder
1/2 tsp. baking soda
1/2 tsp. salt
2 tsps. ground allspice
4 tsps. ground cinnamon
1 tsp. ground nutmeg
1/2 tsp. ground cloves
1 tbsp. vanilla extract
1 tbsp. almond extract
2 cups white sugar
12 egg yolks
1/2 cup molasses
12 egg whites
1/2 cup grape juice
1/2 cup strong brewed coffee

Directions:

1. Wash and dry the raisins and the currants.
2. Wash, dry, pit, and chop the dates.
3. Chop the raisins and the citrus peel.
4. Slice the cherries. Blanch the almonds, and slice them lengthwise.
5. Combine fruits and nuts in large bowl.
6. Grease and line 3 standard Christmas cake pans (these round pans are at least 3 inches deep and come in a set of three sizes- 5, 7, and 9 inch across) with 4 layers of heavy waxed paper, or 3 layers of brown paper.
7. Grease again.
8. Preheat oven to 275 degrees F (135 degrees C).
9. Sift together flour, baking powder, soda, salt, and spices onto a piece of waxed paper.

10. Remove 1 cup of this flour mixture, and combine with fruit and nuts.
11. Mix until fruit is well coated.
12. Cream the butter until fluffy.
13. Add extracts. Gradually add sugar, mixing until creamy.
14. Beat egg yolks until light and lemon-colored, and beat into the butter mixture.
15. Stir in the molasses, and beat together well.
16. Add half of the remaining flour mixture, and blend thoroughly.
17. Beat egg whites until stiff but not dry; fold into batter.
18. Stir in lightly the remaining flour mixture alternately with combined fruit juice and coffee.
19. Add floured fruit and nuts, blending in until fruit is well distributed.
20. Turn batter into prepared cake tins, filling each about 2/3 full and spreading batter evenly.
21. Bake in center of oven.
22. Bake small cake 2 1/2 hours, medium cake 3 1/2 hours, and large cake 4 to 4 1/2 hours.
23. Remove from oven and allow to stand 5 minutes, then turn out on wire rack to cool.

Ice Box Fruitcake

Ingredients:

1 cup chopped pecans
1 cup chopped walnuts
1 cup chopped raisins
1 (4 oz.) jar maraschino cherries, drained and chopped
1 (14 oz.) can sweetened condensed milk
1 (12 oz.) package vanilla wafers, crushed

Directions:

1. In a medium bowl, stir together the pecans, raisins, walnuts, cherries, condensed milk and vanilla wafers.
2. Dough will be very thick, you will need to use your hands.
3. Form dough into a ring shape on top of a dinner plate.
4. Wrap in many layers of plastic wrap and/or aluminum foil.
5. Allow to age in the refrigerator for at least a week.
6. The flavors will have a chance to blend and all of the milk will be absorbed into the cake.

Holiday Bourbon Fruitcake

1 cup chopped candied orange peel
1 cup chopped candied citron
1 cup chopped candied pineapple
1 cup halved red candied cherries
1 cup halved green candied cherries
1 cup dried currants
1 cup raisins
1 cup chopped pitted dates
1 cup chopped walnuts
3/4 cup chopped almonds
1/2 cup orange juice
2/3 cup bourbon whiskey
4 cups all-purpose flour
2 tsps. ground cinnamon
2 tsps. ground nutmeg
1 tsp. ground cloves
1 tsp. ground allspice
1 tsp. ground ginger
2 tsps. unsweetened cocoa powder
1 tsp. baking powder
1/2 tsp. salt
1 1/2 cups butter, room temperature
1 cup packed brown sugar
1/2 cup white sugar
6 egg yolks
3/4 cup applesauce
1/2 cup bourbon whiskey
1 tsp. vanilla extract
1/2 cup molasses
6 egg whites

Directions:

1. On the first day, combine the candied orange peel, candied citron, candied pineapple, red and green candied cherries, currants, raisins, walnuts, and almonds.
2. Combine the orange juice and the 2/3 cup bourbon; pour over the fruit and nuts.
3. Stir and then cover tightly.
4. Let the fruit marinate in a cool place for 1 full day, or at least 20 hours.
5. On the second day, line two 9x5 inch loaf pans with parchment paper or aluminum foil and grease the inside with cooking spray.

6. Combine the flour, cinnamon, nutmeg, cloves, allspice, ginger, cocoa, baking powder, and salt in a large bowl and stir with a whisk to blend.
7. In a separate large bowl, beat the butter, brown sugar, and white sugar until light and fluffy using an electric mixer.
8. Stir in the egg yolks until blended and then mix in the applesauce, the 1/2 cup bourbon, and vanilla until fluffy. Continue stirring, and add the the flour mixture gradually until well combined.
9. Add the molasses and stir to combine. When the batter is thoroughly mixed, gently mix in the fruit and nut mixture with all of its juices.
10. In a separate bowl, whip the egg whites with an electric mixer until they can hold a stiff peak. Fold egg whites into the batter. Divide evenly between the prepared pans. Cover loosely with a towel and let the batter stand overnight in a cool, dry place.
11. On the third day, preheat the oven to 250 degrees F (120 degrees C). Place a large baking pan on the bottom shelf and pour boiling water into it until almost full.
12. Place a baking sheet on the center shelf and place the fruit cakes on the baking sheet.
13. Bake for 2 1/2 hours in the preheated oven. Check the water level and refill if needed.
14. Cover the cakes with a sheet of parchment paper, taking care not to let it touch the shelf. Continue to bake until a knife or toothpick inserted into the center comes out clean, about 1 hour more.
15. Cool fruitcakes in the pans, set over a wire rack. Once cool, remove the cakes from the pans, and leave the parchment paper on.
16. Sprinkle with more bourbon if desired and wrap in aluminum foil.
17. Place in a tin or other sealed container overnight before serving.

Crushed Pineapple Fruitcake

Ingredients:

3/4 cup butter
1 cup white sugar
2 eggs
2 cups all-purpose flour 2 tsps. baking powder
1 tsp. salt
1 tsp. almond extract 3 cups golden raisins
1/2 cup red candied cherries
1 cup candied mixed fruit peel 1 (15 oz.) can crushed pineapple with juice

Directions:

1. Line an angel food pan with parchment paper, and brush with melted butter.
2. Cream butter or margarine, and then beat in sugar.
3. Beat in eggs one at a time, beating well after each addition.
4. Stir in extract.
5. Mix in flour, baking powder, and salt.
6. Stir in raisins, cherries, pineapple, and mixed peel. Allow this to sit overnight in covered bowl.
7. Bake at 300 degrees F (150 degrees C) for 2 1/2 hours with a pan of hot water placed on the lowest rack of your oven during baking. Brush warm cake with some melted butter.

Traditional British Fruitcake

Ingredients:

6 oz. dried prunes chopped
6 oz. dates chopped
8 oz. dark raisins
6 oz. golden raisins
6 oz. currents
3/4 cup butter
1 cup dark brown sugar
3/4 cup molasses
1/2 cup coffee liqueur or 1/2 cup strong black coffee
Zest and juice of 2 oranges
8 oz glace cherries
8 oz candied citrus peel
8 oz toasted pecans roughly chopped
2 tsp. allspice
2 tsp. cinnamon
2 tsp. powdered ginger
1 tsp. cloves
2 tsp. nutmeg
3 tbsp. cocoa
3 eggs
1 1/3 cups all purpose flour
1/2 cup ground hazelnuts or almonds
1/2 tsp baking powder
1/2 tsp baking soda

Directions:

1. In a large saucepan melt the butter over medium heat and add the raisins, dates, prunes, currents, brown sugar, molasses, spices, coffee liqueur (or coffee) and the orange zest and juice.
2. Bring to a gentle boil and very slowly simmer for 10 minutes.
3. Remove from heat and allow to cool for 30-45 minutes.
4. When cool stir in the beaten eggs.
5. Sift together, flour, cocoa, baking powder, baking soda.
6. Add the ground nuts and fold through the boiled mixture. Fold in cherries, citrus peel and pecans. Pour into prepared baking pan. You can decorate the top with additional pecan halves, cherries etc., if you like.
7. Bake at 300 degrees F for 1 ½ to 2 hours depending upon the size of your pan. Mine took the full two hours in a 10 inch spring form pan.

8. The cake should feel firm to the touch at the center and a wooden toothpick inserted into the center should come out clean. The cake should be cooled completely in the pan on a wire rack before removing.
9. At this point you can poke small holes in the top and bottom of the cake with a fork and pour on 4 oz. of dark rum or your favorite whiskey, half on the top, wait ten minutes, then flip it over and pour the remaining half on the bottom.
10. Soak several layers of cheesecloth in additional rum if you like and wrap completely around the cake, then cover with several layers of plastic wrap and store in a Cool place.
11. When serving, you can add a layer of marzipan or if you have decorated the top with fruit and nuts, brush with a simple glaze of equal parts water and sugar boiled together for about 10-15 minutes.

Traditional Scottish Dundee Fruitcake

Ingredients:

1 cup raisins
1 cup dried currants 1/3 cup diced candies mixed fruit peel 1/3 cup candied cherries, quartered 2 tbsps. grated orange zest 1/3 cup all-purpose flour
1 cup butter, softened
1 cup white sugar
4 eggs
1 2/3 cups all-purpose flour
1 tsp. baking powder 1 oz. ground almonds 1/2 cup whole almonds
1 tbsp. corn syrup

Directions:

1. Combine raisins, currants, mixed peel, cherries, and orange rind. Dredge with 1/3 cup flour.
2. Cream butter or margarine and sugar until fluffy.
3. Beat in eggs 1 at a time until light. Combine 1 2/3 cups flour, baking powder, and ground almonds; fold into batter mixture.
4. Mix in fruit.
5. Spread in foil lined 8 x 3 inch round pan. If using a different size pan fill 3/4 full.
6. Bake at 325 degrees F (165 degrees C) for about 1 1/2 hours, until an inserted wooden pick comes out clean. Remove cake from pan.
7. Toast almonds in 350 degrees F (175 degrees C) oven until lightly browned, about 5 minutes. Heat corn syrup, and brush over top surface of hot cake. Place almonds in whatever design you like. After cooling, cake will not be sticky.

Jamaican Fruit Cake

2 cups butter 2 cups white sugar
9 eggs
1/4 cup white rum (optional)
1 tbsp. lime juice
1 tsp. vanilla extract
1 tbsp. almond extract 1 grated zest of one lime 2 pounds chopped dried mixed fruit 2 cups red wine
1 cup dark molasses 2 1/2 cups all-purpose flour 3 tsps. baking powder 1/2 tsp. ground nutmeg 1/2 tsp. ground allspice 1/2 tsp. ground cinnamon 1 pinch salt

Directions:

1. Preheat oven to 350 degrees F (175 degrees C).
2. Grease and flour 2 - 9 inch round cake pans.
3. In a large bowl, cream together the butter and sugar until light and fluffy.
4. Beat in eggs, then add rum, lime juice, vanilla, almond extract, and lime zest.
5. Stir in mixed fruit, wine, and molasses. Sift together flour, baking powder, nutmeg, allspice, cinnamon, and salt. Fold into batter, being careful not to over-mix. Pour into prepared pans.
6. Bake in preheated oven for 80 to 90 minutes, or until a knife inserted into the center comes out clean. Let cool in pan for 10 minutes, then turn out onto a wire rack and cool completely.

White Fruit Cake

Ingredients:

1 1/2 cups candied pineapple chunks 3 cups golden raisins
1 1/2 cups candied cherries
1 cup dried currants 2 oz. candied orange peel 2 oz. candied citron peel 1/2 cup orange juice
2 cups butter 4 cups confectioners' sugar 8 eggs, separated
4 cups pecans, chopped 3 cups sifted all-purpose flour

Directions:

1. Chop pineapple, raisins, and cherries. Combine chopped fruit with currants, orange peel, and citron; soak in orange juice overnight.
2. Preheat oven to 275 degrees F (135 degrees C). Place a small pan of water in the oven. Line one 5x9 inch loaf pan and two 3x8 inch loaf pans with parchment or doubled waxed paper.
3. In a large bowl, cream butter and confectioner's sugar.
4. Stir in beaten egg yolks.
5. Stir in fruit, juice, and pecans.
6. Mix in sifted flour.
7. In a clean bowl, beat the egg whites to peaks. Fold into batter. Fill pans 2/3 full.
8. Bake for 2 to 2 1/2 hours until golden brown, or until toothpick comes out clean when inserted.

Spiced Rum Fruitcake

Ingredients:

For the fruit
3/4 cup dark rum
4 oz. dried apricots, chopped into 1/4- to 1/2-inch pieces (3/4 cup lightly packed)
3 oz. dried apples, chopped into 1/4- to 1/2-inch pieces (1 cup lightly packed)
3 oz. currants or dark raisins (3/4 cup lightly packed)
1/2 tsp. freshly grated orange zest
For the batter
5 oz. (10 Tbs.) unsalted butter, softened; more for the pan
5 oz. (1 cup plus 1 Tbs.) unbleached all-purpose flour
1/2 tsp. ground cinnamon
1/2 tsp. ground allspice
1/4 tsp. ground cardamom
1/8 tsp. freshly grated nutmeg
Pinch of ground cloves
2/3 cup packed dark brown sugar (preferably muscovado)
1/3 cup granulated sugar
3 large eggs, at room temperature
1/2 tsp. pure vanilla extract
1/4 tsp. table salt
3-1/2 oz. crystallized ginger, finely chopped (1/2 cup)
Dark rum, as needed for brushing

Directions:

1. Soak the fruit
2. Put the rum, dried fruit, and orange zest in 2-quart saucepan, cover, and warm over medium heat until hot, 2 to 3 minutes.
3. Remove from the heat and let cool. Refrigerate for a minimum of 24 hours and up to 3 days.
4. Before making the cake, bring the fruit to room temperature and drain, reserving any liquid for basting. (If the fruit was very dry, it may have absorbed all the liquid.)
5. Make the cake
6. Position a rack in the center of the oven and heat the oven to 325 degreesF. Butter an 8-1/2×4-1/2-inch metal loaf pan. Line the pan with two strips of parchment in opposite directions, leaving an overhang for easy removal of the cake.

7. In a medium bowl, whisk the flour with the cinnamon, allspice, cardamom, nutmeg, and cloves. In a stand mixer fitted with the paddle attachment (or in a large bowl with an electric hand mixer), beat the butter and both sugars on medium-high speed until fluffy and no lumps of brown sugar remain, 1 to 2 minutes, stopping to scrape the bowl as needed.
8. Beat in the eggs one at a time, scraping the bowl and mixing for 30 to 60 seconds after each addition.
9. Beat in the vanilla and salt.
10. Add 2 Tbs. of the flour mixture to the bowl and beat briefly. Reserve 2 Tbs. of the flour mixture and add the rest to the batter; beat on low speed for 10 seconds to incorporate the flour and then on medium-high for 1 minute.
11. Combine the crystallized ginger with the drained fruit. Scrape the batter into the center of the bowl. Put the marinated fruit on top of the batter and then sprinkle the reserved flour evenly over the fruit. Using a rubber spatula, fold the fruit into the batter until it's evenly distributed. Scrape the batter into the prepared pan, pressing it in to eliminate air pockets and smoothing the top to make it level.
12. Bake for 15 minutes and then reduce the temperature to 300 degreesF and bake until the center of the cake has risen slightly and a cake tester inserted in the middle comes out clean or with a few moist crumbs, about 1-1/2 hours.
13. Remove the cake and let it cool in its pan on a wire rack for 20 to 30 minutes. Use the parchment overhang to lift the cake from the pan. Place it on the rack, peel down the parchment sides, and cool completely. When cool, brush the cake with 2 to 3 Tbs. of the reserved fruit-soaking liquid or fresh rum.
14. Wrap tightly in plastic and then in foil; store the cake at room temperature for a minimum of 48 hours before serving.
15. If serving within a week of baking, you do not need to baste the cake again. For longer storage, baste once a week with 1 to 2 tbsps. of rum and wrap in fresh plastic and foil. The cake will keep at room temperature for at least 3 weeks.

Fruitcake Cookies

Ingredients:

1 pound white raisins
1 pound red and green candied cherries, chopped 1 pound dates, pitted and chopped 6 slices candied pineapple, chopped
1 cup bourbon whiskey, divided, or as needed
1 cup butter, softened
1 cup brown sugar 3 eggs
1 tbsp. vanilla extract
1 tbsp. ground cinnamon 28 oz. pecans, chopped 3 cups self-rising flour

Directions:

1. Preheat oven to 250 degrees F (120 degrees C).
2. Place raisins, candied cherries, dates, and candied pineapple in a bowl; stir in 1/2 cup bourbon whiskey; set aside to soak.
3. Beat butter and brown sugar together in a large bowl with an electric mixer until light and fluffy.
4. Beat one egg at a time into the butter mixture; beat in vanilla extract and cinnamon with last egg.
5. Stir pecans and fruit mixture into butter mixture; stir in self-rising flour alternately with remaining bourbon whiskey as needed to form a soft dough. Drop tablespoonfuls of dough 2 inches apart onto ungreased baking sheets.
6. Bake in the preheated oven just until cookies begin to look dry, about 30 minutes. Cool cookies on a wire rack; store in a sealed container lined with waxed paper.

Whole Wheat Fruitcake Cookies

Ingredients:

1 cup packed brown sugar
1 cup water
1 cup raisins
2 tbsps. butter 1/2 tsp. salt
1 1/2 cups whole wheat flour 3/4 tsp. baking soda 1/2 tsp. ground ginger
1 tsp. ground cinnamon 1/2 cup dates, pitted and chopped 1/2 cup candied
mixed fruit peel, chopped 1/2 cup chopped nuts 1/2 cup chopped dried
mixed fruit

Directions:

1. Preheat oven to 350 degrees F (175 degrees C).
2. Grease one 5x9 inch loaf pan.
3. In a saucepan over medium heat, cook together the sugar, water, raisins, butter and salt. Remove from heat and allow to cool.
4. Sift together the flour, soda, ginger and cinnamon.
5. Stir into the cooled cooked mixture.
6. Add the chopped dates, mixed peels, nuts and dried fruit.
7. Pour into loaf pan and bake for 1 hour or drop by the tsp. on a cookie sheet and bake for 15 minutes.

Carrot Fruitcake Ring

Ingredients:

1 cup vegetable oil
1 cup white sugar
 1 cup packed brown sugar
4 eggs
3 cups finely grated carrots 2 1/2 cups all-purpose flour 2 tsps. baking powder
1 tsp. baking soda 2 tsps. ground cinnamon
1 tsp. salt
1 cup raisins
1 cup candied cherries, halved
1 cup candied mixed fruit
1 cup dates, pitted and chopped
1 cup coarsely chopped walnuts 1/2 cup all-purpose flour

Directions:

1. Preheat oven to 325 degrees F (165 degrees C).
2. Grease and flour one 10 inch tube pan.
3. Beat the vegetable oil with the white and brown sugars.
4. Beat in the eggs one at a time.
5. Stir in the grated carrots.
6. Add the 2/12 cups flour, baking soda, baking powder, ground cinnamon, and salt.
7. Stir until just moistened.
8. Toss the raisins, candied cherries, candied mixed fruit, chopped dates, and the chopped walnuts with the remaining 1/2 cup flour.
9. Stir to coat.
10. Add fruit and nut mixture to the batter and stir until combined. Pour batter into the prepared pan.
11. Bake at 325 degrees F (165 degrees C) for 1 1/2 hours.

Cherry Fruitcake

Ingredients:

1 lb walnuts or 1 lb pecans
1 lb pitted dates, diced
8 oz. crystallized pineapple
8 oz. candied red cherries
8 oz. green glazed cherries
1 cup sugar
1 tsp. vanilla extract
1 cup all-purpose flour
1 tsp. baking powder
1 tsp. salt
4 whole eggs

Directions:

1. Using a tube pan (line bottom with two greased layers of greased waxed paper, and grease sides of pan); or using two loaf pans or eight mini-loaf pans (line bottom/sides with two greased layers of waxed paper). Be generous with shortening on the layer next to the cake.
2. Cut pineapple, red and green cherries in half; cut dates in 3 pieces.Using hands, combine pineapple, cherries, dates, and pecans in a large bowl.
3. Add sugar, mix well, and set aside for 10 minutes.
4. Beat eggs& vanilla until light and fluffy; pour over fruit and nut mixture. Using hands, mix well. In a separate bowl, combine flour, baking powder, and salt. Pour on above mixture until" syrupy", again, using hands.
5. Preheat oven to 275 degreesF Add cake mixture evenly to pans and pack down tightly.
6. Bake until a toothpick inserted in the middle of the cake comes out clean, approximately 90 minutes for a tube pan; 1 1/4 hr for 2 loaf pans; and check starting after an hour for mini-loaf pans.
7. Remove cake (s) from oven, cool slightly, and remove waxed paper while still warm.

Mango and Mixed Fruit Cake

Ingredients:

1 (15.25 oz.) can mango slices, with juice 1 2/3 cups candied mixed fruit peel
2 tbsps. rum
1 tsp. ground cinnamon
1 tsp. ground nutmeg 1 egg, beaten
1 tsp. vanilla extract
1 cup all-purpose flour
1 tsp. baking powder

Directions:

1. In a medium saucepan, combine mango slices and juice, mixed fruit and rum.
2. Add cinnamon and nutmeg.
3. Stir gently on medium-low heat for 10 to 15 minutes. Remove from heat and let stand until completely cool.
4. Preheat oven to 300 degrees F (150 degrees C).
5. Grease and flour an 8x4 inch loaf pan.
6. Mix together the flour and baking powder; set aside.
7. In a large bowl, combine fruit mixture with egg and vanilla.
8. Stir in flour mixture. Pour into prepared pan.
9. Bake in the preheated oven for 55 to 60 minutes, or until a toothpick inserted into the center of the cake comes out clean. Let cool in pan for 10 minutes, then turn out onto a wire rack and cool completely.

Apple Fruitcake

Ingredients:

2 medium tart apples, peeled and chopped
1/4 cup orange juice
1 cup sugar
2 eggs
1/3 cup canola oil
1/2 tsp. vanilla extract
1-1/2 cups all-purpose flour
1/2 tsp. salt
1/2 tsp. baking powder
1/2 tsp. ground cinnamon
1/4 tsp. baking soda
1/8 tsp. ground nutmeg
1 cup red and/or green candied cherries, quartered
1 package (6 oz.) dried apricots, chopped
1 cup chopped walnuts

Directions:

1. In a small bowl, combine apples and orange juice; set aside. In a large bowl, beat the sugar, eggs, oil and vanilla until well blended. Combine the flour, salt, baking powder, cinnamon, baking soda and nutmeg; add to sugar mixture just until blended. Fold in the cherries, apricots, walnuts and apple mixture.
2. Transfer to a greased and floured 9x5-in. loaf pan.
3. Bake at 350 degrees F for 55-65 minutes or until a toothpick inserted in the center comes out clean. Cool for 10 minutes before removing to a wire rack to cool completely. Cut with a serrated knife.

Christmas Wreath Cake

Ingredients:

1 1/2 cups raisins
1 cup red and green candied cherries
3/4 cup dates, pitted and chopped
3/4 cup candied pineapple, diced
3/4 cup chopped walnuts
1/2 cup flaked coconut
3 cups all-purpose flour
1 tsp. baking powder
1/2 tsp. salt
1 cup butter
1 1/4 cups white sugar
1 tsp. lemon zest
4 eggs
2 tsps. lemon juice

Directions:

1. Preheat oven to 300 degrees F (150 degrees C).
2. Line a tube pan with 2 layers of brown paper or parchment, and grease well.
3. In a large bowl, whisk together flour, baking powder, and salt.
4. Mix in raisins, dates, cherries, pineapple, walnuts, and coconut.
5. Stir until all fruit is coated.
6. In another large bowl, cream the butter with the white sugar.
7. Add lemon rind, lemon juice, and eggs; mix well.
8. Stir in fruit mixture.
9. Spread batter into prepared pan.
10. Bake for 2 hours or until a tester comes out clean.
11. Cool completely on a wire rack.

Graham Cracker Fruitcake

Ingredients:

1 pkg. (16 oz.) graham crackers, finely crushed (about 5 cups crumbs)
1/2 tsp. ground cinnamon
1/2 tsp. ground allspice
1/4 tsp. ground cloves
3/4 cup raisins
1 cup pitted dates, finely chopped
1-1/2 cups mixed candied fruit
1 cup Walnut pieces
1/2 cup orange juice
1/3 cup light corn syrup

Directions:

1. Line 8x5-inch loaf pan with foil, with ends of foil extending over sides of pan; set aside.
2. Mix graham crumbs, spices, raisins, dates, candied fruit and walnuts in large bowl.
3. Mix orange juice and corn syrup until well blended.
4. Add to crumb mixture; stir just until crumbs are moistened.
5. Press graham mixture firmly into prepared pan; cover tightly. Refrigerate at least 2 days.
6. Remove cake from pan just before serving, using foil handles.
7. Discard foil.
8. Let stand until firm.
9. Store, tightly wrapped, in refrigerator.

No Bake Fruit Cake

Ingredients:

1 lb. candied pineapple
1 lb. candied cherries
1 lb. graham crackers
1 lb. coconut
1 lb. nuts
1 lb. raisins
1 lb. butter
1 lb. marshmallows

Directions:

1. Melt the butter and marshmallows together.
2. Chop up fruit and nuts.
3. Crush graham crackers.
4. Mix fruit, nuts, graham crackers, coconut and raisins.
5. Add melted butter and marshmallows.
6. Mix well.
7. Press down well into 2 tube or Bundt pans (ungreased). Let stand for about an hour.
8. Run hot water over the bottom of the pan until the cake comes out.

Traditional Christmas Fruit Cake

Ingredients:

2 cup softened butter
1 1/2 cup sugar
3 cup brown sugar, packed
1/2 cup molasses
8 eggs, beaten
3 cup applesauce
Rind of 1 orange & 1 lemon, grated
Juice from both orange and lemon
1 can crushed pineapple, including juice
2 cups watermelon preserves or citron
1 lb. dates
4 cup raisins
3 cup walnuts or mixed nuts
1 lb. commercial fruit cake mix
Red & green maraschino cherries
1 1/2 cup whole wheat or graham flour
4 1/2 cup white flour
2 tsp. soda
2 tsp. baking powder
2 tsp. cinnamon
1 tsp. allspice
1 tsp. nutmeg
1/2 tsp. cloves
2 tsp. salt

Directions:

1. Mix dates, raisins, nuts, cake mix with whole wheat flour.
2. Cream butter and sugars well.
3. Add molasses and eggs, beat again.
4. Add applesauce, orange and lemon rind and juice, pineapple and juice, beat well.
5. Sift and measure flour and add spices, soda, salt and baking powder, sift into creamed mixture and beat again.
6. Add fruit mixture, blend and pour into pans that have been oiled and lined with wax paper.
7. Bake in slow oven, 300 degrees for 1 1/2 to 2 hours.
8. Time depends on amount of batter put into each pan and size of the pans.

Diabetic Unbaked Fruit Cake

Ingredients:

1 box graham cracker crumbs
1 box (8 oz.) dates
1 sm. jar maraschino cherries
1/2 cup golden raisins
1/2 cup raisins
2 pkg. diced dried fruit mix
1 cup pecans
2 (8 oz.) cans crushed pineapple in own juice

Directions:

1. Drain cherries and discard liquid.
2. Place in small saucepan.
3. Add enough water to cover.
4. Let come to a boil; drain and repeat.
5. Drain again and cover with cold water.
6. Drain and chop dates, pecans, add diced fruit then add graham cracker crumbs.
7. Drain juice from pineapple reserving juice from 1 can.
8. Pour juice and pineapple over fruit and cracker crumbs.
9. Mix thoroughly until all is moistened.
10. Empty mixture in loaf pan sprayed with non-stick spray, cover with wax paper and press firmly in pan.
11. Chill several hours or freeze before cutting.

Fruitcake Rolls

Ingredients:

1 lb. graham crackers, crushed fine
1 lg. bag marshmallows
1 sm. can evaporated milk
1 lb. candied cherries
1/2 lb. candied pineapple
1 cup coconut, packed
1 1/2 cup chopped nuts
1 cup sugar

Directions:

1. Put milk in double boiler over low heat, stir in marshmallows and sugar.
2. Stir until dissolved.
3. Remove boiler and let it cool.
4. Combine remaining ingredients and pour cooled marshmallow mixture over, and mix well.
5. Let cool and make into balls.
6. Roll in cracker crumbs.
7. Wrap separately in wax paper and refrigerate.

Christmas Fruitcake Bars

Ingredients:

6 tbsp. butter
1 cup coconut
1 cup dates, cut into small amount flour so they don't stick
1 1/2 cup graham cracker crumbs
1 cup chopped nuts
2 cup cut up mixed candied fruits
1 can sweetened condensed milk

Directions:

1. Melt butter in 9 x 13 inch pan, then mix in cracker crumbs.
2. Pat down firmly.
3. Sprinkle on coconut next. Distribute candied fruit, then dates, then nuts.
4. Press lightly to level in pan. Pour sweetened condensed milk over all.
5. Bake at 350 degrees for 25 to 30 minutes.
6. Cut into bars or squares when cool.

Fruitcake Squares

Ingredients:

6 tbsp. melted butter
1 1/2 cup crushed graham crackers
2 cup candied cherries or fruit
1 cup coconut
1 cup chopped pecans
1 cup chopped dates
1 can condensed milk

Directions:

1. Melt butter in 9 x 13 inch pan.
2. Sprinkle graham crackers to cover bottom.
3. Press down to form crust.
4. Layer as follows: coconut, dates, candied fruit, nuts.
5. Alternate red and green cherries.
6. Pour can of condensed milk over top.
7. Bake at 350 degrees F for 25 to 30 minu8tes or until done (light brown).

Pressure Cooker Fruitcake

Ingredients:

12 oz. dried fruit and /or mixed fruit
2 cups self rising flour + 1/2 tsp. baking powder
2 cups fruit juice or ice coffee
1 stainless steel short legged trivet

Directions:

1. Rinse Dried Fruit in water to remove any sugar coating (if necessary). Soak fruit in juice overnight.
2. Mix flour, fruit and juice together and pour into greased push pan.
3. Add 1.5 cups of water to your pressure cooker cooking pot and place a trivet.
4. Lower cake into the pressure cooker.
5. Lock on lid and close pressure valve.
6. Cook at high pressure for 1 hour.
7. When beep is heard, allow a 10 minute natural pressure release.

Salted Maple Syrup Fruitcake

Ingredients:

for the fruit cake
1 cup raisins
1/2 cup candied citrus peel
3/4 cup golden sultanas
1/2 cup Medjool dates pitted
1 cup glace cherries
1/2 cup maple-infused prunes
1/2 cup butter, cubed
1 cup sugar
1 cup water
1 tsps. baking soda
2 eggs
1/4 cup brandy
2 cups flour all purpose
1 tsp. baking powder
1 tsps. ground cinnamon
1 tsp. ground ginger
for the salted maple syrup
1 cup water
1/2 cup sugar
1/2 cup maple syrup
2 tbsps. butter
1/2 cup brandy optional
1 pinch sea salt flakes

Directions:

1. Cook the fruit (Except for the cherries), butter, sugar and water until the mixture is dark and sticky.
2. Add the cherries and baking soda and refrigerate over night.
3. The next morning, pre-heat the oven to 350 degrees F.
4. Beat in the eggs and brandy/water into the cooled fruit mixture.
5. Add the flour, baking powder and spices and mix through.
6. Grease and line a cake pan then transfer the cake mix to the prepared cake pan.
7. Place in the oven and bake for 90 mins-2 hours or until a skewer inserted into the center comes out relatively clean.
8. In the meantime, simmer together all the syrup ingredients for 10 minutes then set aside.

9. When the cake comes out of the oven, pour over the syrup then allow to soak in overnight.

Paleo Fruitcake

Ingredients:

1½ cups blanched almond flour (not almond meal)
½ tsp. celtic sea salt
½ tsp. baking soda
½ cup dates (remove pits) and chopped
½ cup raisins
½ cup dried cherries
1 cup walnuts, chopped
4 large eggs
2 tbsps. coconut oil
1 tbsp. coconut sugar
1 tbsp. vanilla extract
1 tbsp. orange zest
1 tbsp. lemon zest

Directions:

1. In a large bowl, combine almond flour, salt and baking soda
2. Stir in dried fruit and nuts
3. In a medium bowl, combine eggs, oil, coconut sugar, vanilla and citrus zest
4. Stir wet ingredients into dry
5. Scoop batter into 2 greased mini loaf pans
6. Bake fruitcakes at 350 degrees F for 20-30 minutes
7. Cool and serve

Texas Brandied Fruitcake

Ingredients:

1-1/2 pounds (about 3 cups) mixed diced candied fruit
(dates, dried cherries, candied pineapple, etc.
2-1/2 cups chopped pecans
1 15-oz. package golden raisins
1/2 cup brandy, for soaking fruit
2 tbsps. butter, softened
2 tbsps. fine dry breadcrumbs
3 cups all-purpose flour
1 tsp. baking powder
1/2 tsp. salt
1/4 tsp. ground allspice
1/2 tsp. cinnamon
1 cup additional butter, softened
2 cups firmly packed light brown sugar
4 eggs
3/4 cup brewed coffee
2 cups additional brandy, for sprinkling
Additional whole pecans, candied fruit, etc., for decorating

Directions:

1. In a large bowl, combine the candied fruit, pecans, raisins and 1/2 cup brandy. Toss to mix thoroughly, cover, and let stand for 3 to 5 hours at room temperature.
2. Preheat oven to 325 degrees F.
3. Using 1 tbsp. butter for each, butter two 9-inch loaf pans.
4. Sprinkle each with 1 tbsp. of the breadcrumbs, and rotate to coat evenly.
5. Sift together the flour, baking powder, salt, allspice and cinnamon.
6. In the large bowl of an electric mixer, cream 1 cup butter with the brown sugar.
7. Add the eggs, one at a time, beating well after each addition, and continue to beat until light and fluffy.
8. Add the flour mixture alternately with the coffee, stirring after each addition, until batter is just blended.
9. Pour batter over the fruit mixture and blend thoroughly.
10. Spoon batter into prepared pans.
11. Bake in preheated oven for 1-1/2 hours (or 1 hour 45 minutes for a single round fruitcake) or until a cake tester inserted in center comes out clean.

12. Let cakes cool in pans for 20 minutes, and then turn out onto racks, and cool completely.
13. Place each cake on a large sheet of aluminum foil.
14. Sprinkle each cake with 1/4 cup brandy.
15. Wrap each cake tightly in the aluminum foil, sealing well.
16. Store in a cool dark place.
17. After seven days, unwrap the cakes and sprinkle each with an additional 1/4 cup brandy. Rewrap.
18. Repeat this procedure each week for the next two weeks.
19. Let the cakes sit for a final week before serving.
20. Makes two 9x5-inch fruitcakes (or one 10-inch round fruitcake).
21. Don't just dump the brandy over the cake.
22. Slowly let the brandy drip onto the cake so that it is absorbed.
23. If you like, use a toothpick to make small holes in the surface of the cake.

Tropical Fruitcake

Ingredients:

1 1/2 cups all-purpose flour
1/2 tsp. baking powder
1/4 tsp. baking soda
1/2 cup butter
3/4 cup packed brown sugar
2 eggs
1/4 cup rum
1/4 cup pineapple juice
2 tbsps. light corn syrup
1 tsp. grated fresh ginger
1 tsp. vanilla
1 3/4 cups mixed dried tropical fruit
1/2 cup chopped macadamia nuts
1/3 cup rum
1/4 cup rum

Directions:

1. Grease and lightly flour eight 1-cup fluted tube pans or six 4-1/2x2-1/2x1-1/2-inch individual loaf pans and set pans aside.
2. In a medium bowl combine flour, baking powder, and baking soda; set aside.
3. In a large bowl beat butter with an electric mixer on medium to high speed for 30 seconds, add brown sugar; beat until combined.
4. Add eggs, one at a time, beating on medium speed until combined.
5. The batter may appear curdled.
6. Combine 1/4 cup rum, 1/4 cup pineapple juice, corn syrup, ginger, and vanilla.
7. Add flour mixture and rum mixture alternately to butter mixture, beating on low speed after each addition just until combined.
8. Fold in fruit bits and nuts.
9. Spread batter in prepared pan.
10. Bake in a 325 degree oven for 20 to 25 minutes for fluted tube pans or 30 to 35 minutes for loaf pans or until a toothpick inserted into centers comes out clean.
11. Cool cakes in pans on wire racks for 10 minutes.
12. Remove from pans; cool at least 1 hour on racks.
13. Poke holes in cakes using a wooden toothpick or bamboo skewer.

14. Soak eight or six 8-inch-square pieces of double thickness 100-percent cotton cheesecloth with the 1/3 cup rum or pineapple juice and wrap each cake in rum- or juice-soaked cheesecloth.
15. Wrap each cake tightly in foil or seal in a plastic bag.
16. Chill in refrigerator for 24 hours.
17. Remove foil or remove cakes from bags; drizzle with 1/4 cup rum or pineapple juice.
18. Rewrap with foil or return to plastic bags and refrigerate at least 24 hours.
19. Remove cheesecloth before serving.
20. Sprinkle with sifted powdered sugar.

White Chocolate Fruitcake Fudge

Ingredients:

1 tbsp. butter
12 oz. white chocolate morsels
1/2 cup sweetened condensed milk
1/2 tsp. sea salt
1/2 cup chopped pecans
1½ cups chopped candied fruit
1/4 tsp. rum extract

Directions:

1. Line loaf pan with foil and generously grease with butter.
2. Layer a handful of nuts and fruit on the bottom of pan.
3. Set aside.
4. In 3.5 quart pot over medium/low; combine butter, white chocolate, condensed milk and salt.
5. Heat and stir until chocolate is melted and smooth.
6. Remove from heat.
7. Stir in rum extract, fruit and pecans.
8. Transfer to prepared loaf pan and spread evenly, gently pressing down.
9. Refrigerate overnight.
10. Remove from pan. Carefully peel off foil.
11. Cut into squares.

Christmas Cherry Fruitcake

1 cup white sugar
1 cup butter
2 eggs
1/2 cup orange juice
2 cups all-purpose flour
1 tsp. baking powder
12 oz. golden raisins
8 oz. halved glace cherries

Directions:

1. Preheat oven to 300 degrees F (150 degrees C).
2. Grease and line with parchment paper one 9x5 inch loaf pan.
3. Cream butter or margarine and sugar together until light and fluffy.
4. Add beaten eggs and orange juice and mix well.
5. Sift flour and baking powder.
6. Reserve 1/3 cup of flour mixture and toss with raisins and cherries (this will keep them from sinking to the bottom of the cake).
7. Add flour mixture to batter and blend.
8. Add floured raisins and cherries to dough and mix until just combined.
9. Pour batter into prepared pan.
10. Bake at 300 degrees F (150 degrees C) for 2-1/2 hours.
11. Don't serve until several days old.
12. Wrap the cake in plastic wrap or foil and store in a sealed tin.

Fruit Cake Donuts

Ingredients:

Canola oil, for frying
2 cups pancake mix
1 cup milk
1 fruit cake, sliced and cut into 2-3 inch cubes
Powdered sugar, for garnish

Directions:

1. In a deep fryer or Dutch oven with oil, heat canola oil to 350 degrees F.
2. In a mixing bowl, whisk together the pancake mix and milk.
3. Let rest for 5 minutes.
4. Using a fork, dip each piece of fruit cake into the batter and coat on all sides.
5. Drop the battered fruit cake into the oil a few at a time, and brown on one side, for about 20-30 seconds.
6. Flip with a fork or slotted spoon and brown the other side, about 20 seconds.
7. Remove with a slotted spoon and drain on paper towels.

Glazed Fruitcake Donuts

Ingredients:

1/2 cup unbleached all-purpose flour
1/2 cup whole wheat flour
¼ cup sugar
1 tsp. baking powder
1/8 tsp. baking soda
¼ tsp. salt
½ tsp. cinnamon
½ tsp. nutmeg
¼ tsp. allspice
¼ tsp. mace
1/8 tsp. cloves
1 tbsp. salted butter, softened
1 ½ tsp molasses
¼ c milk
¼ c brandy
½ tsp pure vanilla extract
½ tsp orange zest
1 egg
½ cup mixed dried fruits (chopped apricots, raisins, currants, golden raisins, etc.)
2 tbsp. walnuts, chopped
Glaze Ingredients:
¾ cup sugar
½ cup brandy
1 tsp pure vanilla extract Instructions

Directions:

1. Preheat your oven to 350F.
2. In a medium bowl, mix flour, sugar, baking powder, baking soda, salt, and spices.
3. Melt butter and molasses together in a small bowl in the microwave.
4. Set aside to cool slightly.
5. In a large bowl, add milk, brandy, vanilla, and orange zest.
6. Add egg, and beat until incorporated.
7. Stir in flour mixture until moistened.
8. Add fruit and nuts and mix until just combined.
9. Spoon batter into greased baked donut pans, filling ¾ of the way full.
10. Bake for 8-10 minutes, until firm.

11. Remove from pan to a wire rack and cool completely before making glaze.

Glaze Directions:

1. Combine the glaze ingredients in a small saucepan over medium heat.
2. Stir until sugar is dissolved. Increase heat to high.
3. Simmer, stirring, for 3 minutes. (Glaze should be just starting to turn from clear to opaque when it is done.)
4. Let the glaze cool slightly.
5. Dip the slightly cooled donuts into the still runny glaze, and place on a wire rack to let the glaze set up.

Caribbean Black Fruitcake

Fruit Ingredients:

1 3/4 cups whole raw almonds, coarsely chopped
1 3/4 cups dried cherries, coarsely chopped
1 3/4 cups prunes, coarsely chopped
1 1/2 cups dark rum, plus 4 tbsps. for brushing
1 1/2 cups raisins, coarsely chopped
1 1/2 cups ruby port
1 1/4 cups currants
3/4 cup candied orange peel, coarsely chopped

Cake Ingredients:

3 cups all-purpose flour
2 tsps. kosher salt
1 tbsp. baking powder
1/2 tsp. ground cinnamon
1/2 tsp. ground clove
1/2 tsp. ground nutmeg
4 sticks (1 lb.) unsalted butter, at room temperature
2 1/4 cups packed light brown sugar
6 large eggs, at room temperature
2 tsps. vanilla extract
3/4 cup burnt sugar syrup

Fruit Directions:

1. Combine all ingredients in a 3-quart container with a tightfitting lid and mix well. Cover tightly and store in a dark, cool, dry place for 1 week.

Cake Directions:

1. Heat the oven to 300 degrees F and arrange a rack in the middle.
2. Coat two 9-by-5-inch loaf pans with butter; set aside.
3. Combine flour, salt, baking powder, cinnamon, clove, and nutmeg in a large bowl and whisk to aerate and break up any lumps. Set aside.
4. Place butter and sugar in the bowl of a stand mixer fitted with a paddle attachment, and beat on medium speed until pale yellow, about 3 minutes.
5. Scrape down the sides of the bowl, and return the mixer to medium speed.
6. Add eggs one at a time, letting each mix in fully before adding the next.

7. Add vanilla. Scrape down the sides of the bowl and return the mixer to low speed.
8. Add flour mixture, macerated fruit and nuts along with any unabsorbed liquid, and burnt sugar, and mix until just combined.
9. Divide batter evenly between the prepared pans (the pans will be completely full).
10. Bake until a cake tester comes out clean (the cake centers will be very moist), about 2 hours.
11. Let cool 30 minutes in the pans on a wire rack.
12. Turn cakes out onto the rack, and brush each with 2 tbsps. dark rum. Cool completely before slicing and eating, or aging.
13. To age, store each cooled cake in a re-sealable plastic bag at room temperature for up to 2 months.
14. A dark cupboard or pantry is ideal, but do not refrigerate, as the moisture level will change the texture.

Spiced Dark Fruitcake

Ingredients:

3 cups all-purpose flour
2 tsps. baking soda
1 tsp. ground allspice
1 tsp. ground cinnamon
1 tsp. freshly grated nutmeg
1/2 tsp. fine salt
3 sticks (12 oz.) unsalted butter, at room temperature
2 cups packed dark brown sugar
6 large eggs, at room temperature
1/2 cup dark molasses (not blackstrap)
3 tbsps. freshly grated lemon zest (from 3 to 4 lemons)
1/2 cup brandy
2 cups dried, unsulfured apricots, coarsely chopped
2 cups almonds, coarsely chopped
1 1/2 cups golden raisins, also known as sultanas
1 1/2 cups Medjool dates, coarsely chopped
1 cup candied orange zest, coarsely chopped

Directions:

1. Heat the oven to 300 degrees F and arrange a rack in the middle.
2. Coat two 9-by-5-inch loaf pans with butter and flour; set aside.
3. Combine flour, baking soda, allspice, cinnamon, nutmeg, and salt in a large bowl and whisk to aerate and break up any lumps; set aside.
4. Place butter in the bowl of a stand mixer fitted with the paddle attachment and beat on medium-high speed until pale yellow, about 3 minutes.
5. Add brown sugar, and continue beating until fluffy, about 3 minutes.
6. Add eggs one at a time, letting each mix in fully before adding the next.
7. Scrape down the sides of the bowl.
8. Return the mixer to medium-high speed, add molasses and lemon zest, and beat until combined.
9. Reduce speed to low and mix in 1/3 of the flour mixture.
10. Add 1/4 cup of the brandy, another 1/3 of the flour mixture, the remaining 1/4 cup brandy, and finally the last 1/3 of the flour.
11. Mix until flour is just incorporated and batter is smooth.
12. Remove the bowl from the mixer and fold in remaining ingredients.
13. Divide batter evenly between the prepared pans.

14. Bake until a toothpick inserted in the center comes out clean, about 1 1/2 hours.
15. Let cool on a wire rack for at least 1 hour before removing from the pan. Turn cakes out onto the rack and cool completely before slicing and eating, or aging.
16. To age, brush each cake with 1/4 cup brandy, and then completely bury each in 4 pounds of powdered sugar for up to 4 months.

German Stollen Fruitcake

Ingredients:

1 cup dark and golden raisins,
1/4 cup candied lemon peel
1/8 cup candied orange peel
2 oz. (50 ml or 1 miniature bottle) dark rum
1 envelope yeast
1/2 cup milk
1/3 cup sugar
4 cup all-purpose flour
1 egg
1 tsp. vanilla extract
2 tbsps. lemon zest (zest from 1 lemon)
1/4 tsp salt
1/4 tsp. ground nutmeg
1/4 tsp. ground cardamom
7/8 cup sweet, unsalted butter
2/3 cup flour
1/3 cup whole almonds (blanched, peeled and chopped)
1/2 cup melted butter
1/2 cup powdered sugar (for dusting)

Directions:

1. Soak raisins, candied fruit and almonds in rum overnight, stirring occasionally.
2. Dissolve yeast in warm milk and a pinch of sugar.
3. Proof for 10 minutes, or until bubbles form.
4. Mix flour, egg, yeast mixture, sugar, lemon peel and salt with a spoon or in a stand mixer using the dough hook for several minutes.
5. The dough should just come together and not be very smooth yet. Remove from bowl and set aside while you do the next step.
6. Cream the butter and 2/3 cup flour with the nutmeg and cardamom until smooth.
7. Add the yeast dough back to the bowl and work the dough with a dough hook or by hand until the butter and flour mixture is completely incorporated. This should yield a smooth dough.
8. Let dough rest, covered, for 30 minutes.
9. Turn dough out onto tabletop or lightly floured board.
10. Knead in fruit and chopped almonds. Let rest for 15 minutes.

11. Return dough to floured board and form into a rectangle with two high sides and a dip in the middle.
12. Fold 1/3 of the dough over to the middle, filling the dip. Pat into a stollen shape.
13. Fold a piece of aluminum foil several times on the two long ends to build walls for your stollen, to help hold its shape while baking.
14. Let stollen rise for 30 minutes in a warm place.
15. Preheat oven to 350 F. Dot the top of the stollen with butter.
16. Bake loaves for 35 - 45 minutes, or until loaves are golden and done. Cover with foil if it begins to brown too much.
17. Brush warm loaf with butter and dust thickly with powdered sugar.
18. Cool on ?rack.
19. Wrap tightly in foil and keep in a cool place for 2 to 3 weeks to ripen.

Grand Marnier Fruitcake

Ingredients:

3 cup golden raisins
1½ cup candied citrus peel
¾ cup coarsely chopped dark raisins
¾ cup coarsely chopped pitted dried dates
? cup coarsely chopped pitted prunes
½ cup coarsely chopped glacé apricots
? cup coarsely chopped glacé pineapple
½ cup slivered almonds
½ cup coarsely chopped walnuts
1 tbsp. finely grated orange rind
½ cup superfine sugar
¼ cup orange juice
½ cup Grand Marnier
2 stick butter
½ cup firmly packed light brown sugar
5 eggs
2 cup all-purpose flour
2 tbsp. Grand Marnier
2 lb. ready-made white fondant
1 egg white
½ cup confectioners' sugar
10-inch round covered cake board
Decorative ribbon
Silver drageés

Directions:

1. Combine fruit, nuts, and rind in large bowl.
2. Cook sugar in large frying pan over low heat, without stirring, until it begins to melt, then stir until sugar is melted and browned lightly.
3. Remove from heat, slowly stir in juice; return to low heat, stir until sugar dissolves (do not boil).
4. Stir in liqueur.
5. Pour syrup over fruit mixture.
6. Cover with plastic wrap; store mixture in a cool, dark place for 10 days, stirring every day.
7. Preheat oven to 300 degrees F.

8. Line base and sides of deep 9-inch round or deep 8-inch square cake pan with two layers of parchment paper, extending paper 2 inches above edge of pan.
9. Beat butter and brown sugar in small bowl with electric mixer until just combined; beat in eggs, one at a time.
10. Stir butter mixture into fruit mixture.
11. Mix in sifted flour; spread mixture into pan.
12. Tap pan firmly on counter to settle mixture into pan; level cake mixture with wet spatula.
13. Bake cake about 3 1/2 hours. Remove cake from oven, brush with extra liqueur; cover hot cake with foil, then turn upside down to cool overnight.
14. Trim top of cake with sharp knife to ensure it sits flat when turned upside down.
15. Mix a little fondant and cold water to a sticky paste.
16. Spread about 2 tbsps. of this mixture into the center of a sheet of parchment paper about 2 inches larger than the cake; position cake upside down on paper.
17. Using spatula and small pieces of fondant, patch any holes on cake.
18. Brush egg white evenly over cake. Knead white fondant on surface dusted with confectioners' sugar until smooth; roll to 1/4-inch thickness.
19. Lift icing onto cake with rolling pin, smoothing icing over cake with hands dusted with confectioners' sugar.
20. Using sharp knife, cut excess icing away from base of cake.
21. Mix scraps of fondant and cold water to a sticky paste.
22. Spread about 2 tbsps. of paste in center of board; center cake on prepared board.
23. Move the cake to the correct position on the board; using sharp craft knife or scalpel, carefully cut away excess parchment paper extending around base of cake.
24. Secure ribbon around cake using pins (remove before cutting cake).
25. Push drageés gently into icing in the design of your choice.

Stout Fruitcake

Ingredients:

1 cup unsalted butter
12 oz. prunes
8 oz. golden raisins
8 oz. currants
1¼ cup stout
2? cup all-purpose flour
½ tsp. baking powder
¼ tsp. nutmeg
¼ tsp. ground cinnamon
1¼ cup light-brown sugar
2 eggs

Directions:

1. Heat oven to 300 degrees F. Brush a 9-by-4 1/2-inch loaf pan with butter. Line pan with parchment; brush with butter.
2. Set aside.
3. Combine the prunes, raisins, and currants in a medium bowl.
4. Add 1/2 cup stout, and let stand.
5. Sift flour, baking powder, nutmeg, and cinnamon.
6. In the bowl of an electric mixer fitted with the paddle attachment, cream butter and sugar until fluffy, about 3 minutes.
7. Add eggs, one at a time, mixing well after each, scraping down sides twice.
8. Add dry ingredients in two additions; mix just to combine.
9. Fold in fruit mixture.
10. Pour batter into pan.
11. Bake until dark brown and set and a cake tester inserted into the middle of cake comes out clean, about 3 1/2 hours. (Cracks will appear on top of cake.)
12. Remove from oven; sprinkle with 1/2 cup stout.
13. Let stand on wire rack 30 minutes. Remove from pan; discard parchment; let cool completely.
14. Wrap in cheesecloth or muslin. Douse fruitcake with remaining 1/4 cup stout.
15. Store in a cool, dark, dry place, dousing with 1/4 cup stout once a week for at least 1 month before serving.

Golden Glacé Fruit Cake

Ingredients:

5 oz. glacé pear
5 oz. red and green glacé cherries
5 oz. glacé peach
4 oz. glacé ginger
4 oz. glacé figs
? cup brandy or orange-flavored liqueur
8 oz. unsalted butter
1 cup superfine sugar
4 eggs
1? cup all-purpose flour
1 cup ground almonds

Directions:

1. Preheat oven to 300 degrees F. Line base and side of deep 8-inch round cake pan with two layers of parchment paper, extending paper 2 inches over edge of pan.
2. Combine fruit and 1/2 cup of the brandy in large bowl.
3. Beat butter and sugar in small bowl with electric mixer until combined.
4. Beat in eggs one at a time.
5. Add butter mixture to fruit mixture; mix well.
6. Stir in sifted flour and ground almonds, in two batches.
7. Spread mixture into pan; smooth top.
8. Bake cake about 3 hours. Brush hot cake with remaining brandy. While still hot, cover cake, still in its pan, tightly with foil; cool in pan.

Chocolate Fruit Cake

Fruit Cake Ingredients:

1¾ lb. canned pitted black cherries in syrup
1 cup dark raisins
¾ cup finely chopped pitted dried dates
½ cup golden raisins
½ cup finely chopped pitted prunes
1 cup dried figs
1 cup marsala wine
1 cup pecans
1½ stick butter
2 tsp. finely grated orange rind
1¼ cup firmly packed dark brown sugar
3 eggs
1¼ cup all-purpose flour
½ cup self-rising flour
2 tbsp. cocoa powder
2 tsp. pie spice
3 oz. semi-sweet chocolate

Ganache Ingredients:

7 oz. semi-sweet chocolate
½ cup heavy cream

Directions:

1. Drain cherries; reserve 1/3 cup syrup.
2. Quarter cherries.
3. Combine cherries with remaining fruit, 3/4 cup of the Marsala, and reserved cherry syrup in large bowl. Cover; stand overnight.
4. Preheat oven to 300 degrees F.
5. Grease deep 9-inch round cake pan; line with two layers of parchment paper, extending paper 2 inches over edge of pan.
6. Process half the nuts until ground finely; chop the remaining nuts coarsely.
7. Beat butter, rind, and sugar in small bowl with electric mixer until combined; beat in eggs, one at a time.
8. Mix butter mixture into fruit mixture; stir in sifted dry ingredients, chocolate, and ground and chopped nuts.
9. Spread mixture into pan.

10. Bake cake about 3 hours. Brush hot cake with remaining marsala, cover with foil; cool in pan.
11. Make ganache:
12. Stir ingredients in small saucepan over low heat until smooth. Refrigerate, stirring occasionally, about 20 minutes or until spreadable.
13. Spread cake with ganache; top with chocolate decoration.
14. Dust with sifted confectioners' sugar to serve, if you like.

Old English Fruitcake

Ingredients:

6 oz dried prunes chopped
6 oz dates chopped
8 oz dark raisins
6 oz golden raisins
6 oz currents
¾ cup butter
1 cup dark brown sugar
¾ cup molasses
½ cup coffee liqueur or ½ cup strong black coffee
Zest and juice of 2 oranges
8 oz glace cherries
8 oz candied citrus peel
8 oz toasted pecans roughly chopped
2 tsp allspice
2 tsp cinnamon
2 tsp powdered ginger
1 tsp cloves
2 tsp nutmeg
3 tbsp. cocoa
3 eggs
1 1/3 cups all purpose flour
½ cup ground hazelnuts or almonds
½ tsp baking powder
½ tsp baking soda
US Customary - Metric

Directions:

1. In a large saucepan melt the butter over medium heat and add the raisins, dates, prunes, currents, brown sugar, molasses, spices, coffee liqueur (or coffee) and the orange zest and juice.
2. Bring to a gentle boil and very slowly simmer for 10 minutes.
3. Remove from heat and allow to cool for 30-45 minutes.
4. When cool stir in the beaten eggs.
5. Sift together, flour, cocoa, baking powder, baking soda.
6. Add the ground nuts and fold through the boiled mixture. Fold in cherries, citrus peel and pecans. Pour into prepared baking pan. You can decorate the top with additional pecan halves, cherries etc., if you like.

7. Bake at 300 degrees F for 1 ½ to 2 hours depending upon the size of your pan. Mine took the full two hours in a 10 inch spring form pan.
8. The cake should feel firm to the touch at the center and a wooden toothpick inserted into the center should come out clean. The cake should be cooled completely in the pan on a wire rack before removing.
9. At this point you can poke small holes in the top and bottom of the cake with a fork and pour on 4 oz. of dark rum or your favorite whiskey, half on the top, wait ten minutes, then flip it over and pour the remaining half on the bottom.
10. Soak several layers of cheesecloth in additional rum if you like and wrap completely around the cake, then cover with several layers of plastic wrap and store in a cool place.
11. When serving, you can add a layer of marzipan or if you have decorated the top with fruit and nuts, brush with a simple glaze of equal parts water and sugar boiled together for about 10-15 minutes.

Mexican Fruitcake

Ingredients:

2 cups all-purpose flour
2 cups sugar
2 large eggs
2 tsps. baking soda
1 (16 oz.) can crushed pineapple in juice
1 cup walnuts, coarsely chopped
Cream Cheese Frosting
1 (8 oz.) package cream cheese, softened
1 stick margarine
1 tsp. vanilla extract
2 cups powdered sugar

Directions:

1. Make cake Preheat oven to 350 degrees F.
2. In large bowl, stir all cake ingredients together by hand.
3. Spread evenly in 9- x 13-inch glass baking dish and bake until toothpick inserted into center comes out clean, about 35 minutes.
4. While cake is baking, make frosting In large bowl, using electric mixer, beat cream cheese, margarine, and vanilla until smooth.
5. Add sugar and continue to beat until well combined. Pour frosting over the cake immediately upon taking the cake out of the oven.
6. Cool the frosted cake in the refrigerator.

Christmas Chestnut Fruitcake

Ingredients:

1½ cups blanched almond flour (not almond meal)
½ tsp. Celtic sea salt
½ tsp. baking soda
½ cup dates (remove pits) and chopped
½ cup raisins
½ cup dried cherries
1 cup walnuts, chopped
4 large eggs
2 tbsps. coconut oil
1 tbsp. coconut sugar
1 tbsp. vanilla extract
1 tbsp. orange zest
1 tbsp. lemon zest

Directions:

1. In a large bowl, combine almond flour, salt and baking soda
2. Stir in dried fruit and nuts
3. In a medium bowl, combine eggs, oil, coconut sugar, vanilla and citrus zest
4. Stir wet ingredients into dry
5. Scoop batter into 2 greased mini loaf pans
6. Bake fruitcakes at 350 degrees F for 20-30 minutes
7. Cool and serve

Gingered Christmas Fruitcake

Cake Ingredients:

2.8 oz. dried figs, chopped
2.3 oz. dried cranberries
2.3 oz. dates, chopped
1.75 oz. glace cherries, chopped
1 oz mixed candied peel
1.75 oz. raisins
1.75 oz. sultanas
1.75 oz. currants
3.5 oz. crystallised ginger, chopped
1.75 oz. stem ginger, finely chopped
Zest of 1 + juice 1/2 orange
Zest of 1 lemon
1tbsp stem ginger syrup
4 tbsp. rum/brandy/sherry (plus extra for feeding)
140g (1/3 + ¼ cups) softened butter
140g (2/3 cup + 2tbsp) light brown soft sugar
1.5 tbsp. treacle
2 eggs
1 1/2 cups plain flour
40g (1/3 cup) ground almonds
1 1/2 tsp ground ginger
1/2 tsp. ground cinnamon
1/2 tsp. ground nutmeg
1/4 tsp. ground cardamom
1/8 tsp. ground cloves
pinch salt
Royal icing
3 tbsp. apricot jam or marmalade
17.5oz marzipan
2 large egg whites
4 cups powdered sugar, sifted
1½ tsp. lemon juice
1 tsp. glycerine (optional, but stops the icing from set rock solid)

Decoration Ingredients:

1 small orange
a couple of small pine cones
1 egg white

2 tsp. caster sugar
1 handful fresh cranberries
2 sprigs fresh rosemary
2 bay leaves
Granulated sugar
Cinnamon sticks
Star anise
Icing
Sugar

Directions:

1. The day before you want to bake the cake, mix all of the dried fruits together in a large bowl and stir in the orange and lemon zests, orange juice, stem ginger syrup and alcohol, cover and leave to soak overnight.
2. The following day, preheat the oven to 300F/150C.
3. Grease a deep 15cm/6in round cake tin and line the base and sides with a double thickness of baking parchment, making sure that it comes a good 10cm above the top of the tin.
4. Cream together the butter, sugar and treacle with an electric mixer until pale, then add the eggs one at a time, beating well after each addition.
5. Add a spoonful of the flour if the mixture looks like it is about to split.
6. Sift together the flour, ground almonds, spices and salt then fold into the creamed mixture followed by the soaked fruit; combine well.
7. Scrape the cake mixture into the prepared tin and level the surface.
8. Bake for 2 hours to 2 hours 45 minutes until a skewer inserted into the center comes out clean; cover with tin foil if it starts to get too dark.
9. When the cake is ready, sprinkle a couple of tbsps. of your choice of alcohol over the top then leave it to cool completely in the tin.
10. When cold, remove it from the tin and peel off the parchment.
11. Wrap in tin foil and store for up to three weeks, feeding it with alcohol a couple of times a week.
12. When you are ready to ice the cake, trim the top to level it if necessary, turn it upside down and place it on a cake board or serving platter.
13. Use a little of the marzipan to fill in any holes in the cake and gaps between the cake and board.
14. Gently warm the jam in a microwave or in a small pan on the stove until it is runny then brush a thin layer of it all over the cake, avoiding any bits.
15. Knead the marzipan a little to warm it up, then roll it out on a surface dusted with icing sugar to a large circle about 5mm thick.
16. Drape the marzipan over the top of the cake, dust your hands with icing sugar and smooth the marzipan over the top and sides to cover the cake completely, working out any folds and wrinkles.

17. Trim to make a neat edge.
18. At this point you can leave the cake to dry out for a couple of days if you like, or proceed straight to making the icing.
19. Place the egg whites in a large, very clean bowl and whisk until they are just foamy.
20. Stir in the icing sugar a spoonful at a time with a spatula then add the lemon juice and glycerine if using.
21. Whisk with an electric mixer until it is very thick and white and stands up in stiff peaks.
22. Cover the top and sides of the cake with the royal icing, smoothing it with a palette knife. Try to level the top but don't worry about getting it completely smooth, it should be a slightly rough finish.
23. Allow the icing to dry a little before decorating. While it is drying make the dried orange slices.
24. Heat the oven to it's lowest setting.
25. Cut the orange into thin slices and lay them on a wire rack; place the rack in the oven and bake for a couple of hours until dried.
26. They will still feel a little bit tacky. remove from the oven and leave to cool.
27. To make the sugared cranberries, rosemary and bay leaves, beat the egg white with the 2tsp sugar until just frothy.
28. Pour some granulated sugar in a shallow bowl. Dip the cranberries in the egg white and shake off any excess, allow to dry a little then roll in the sugar, place on a tray and leave to dry for at least half an hour; repeat with the rosemary and bay leaves.
29. Arrange the pine cones, a couple of the dried orange slices, the sugared cranberries, rosemary and bay leaves and a few cinnamon sticks and star anise on the top of the cake.
30. Dust with a little icing sugar.

Creole Christmas Fruitcake

Syrup Ingredients:

2 cups granulated sugar
2 cups water
Strips of zest of 2 lemons (about 3 tbsps.)
Juice of 2 lemons (about 1/4 cup)

Cake Ingredients:

1 lb. of a combination of dried fruits, such as blueberries, cranberries, cherries, raisins, and chopped apricots
1 lb. (4 sticks) unsalted butter, at room temperature
2 1/4 cups granulated sugar
4 oz. almond paste
8 large eggs
1 cup Grand Marnier
4 cups bleached all-purpose flour
2 tsps. baking powder
1/4 tsp. salt
1/4 tsp. ground cinnamon
1/8 tsp. freshly grated nutmeg
1 cup slivered blanched almonds
1 cup pecan pieces
1 cup walnut pieces
1/2 cup bourbon

Whiskey Sauce Directions:

1. Make a simple syrup by combining the sugar and water in medium-size heavy-bottomed saucepan over medium-high heat.
2. Add the lemon zest and juice and bring to a boil, stirring to dissolve the sugar.
3. Boil for 2 minutes and remove from the heat.
4. Combine the dried fruits together in a large mixing bowl.
5. Pour the simple syrup over them, toss to coat, and let steep for 5 minutes.
6. Strain and serve the syrup.
7. Cream the butter, sugar, and almond paste together in the bowl of an electric mixer fitted with a paddle at low speed, occasionally scraping down the sides of the bowl.
8. Beat until the mixture is fluffy and smooth, about 2 minutes.

9. Add the eggs one at a time, mixing in between each addition on low speed and scraping down the sides of the bowl as necessary.
10. Add 1/2 cup of the Grand Marnier and mix to incorporate.
11. Combine the flour, baking powder, salt, cinnamon, and nutmeg in a medium-size mixing bowl and blend well.
12. Add this mixture 1/2 cup at a time to the butter mixture with the mixer on low speed, each time mixing until smooth, about 2 minutes.
13. Scrape down the sides of the bowl as necessary.
14. The batter will be thick.
15. Add the warm fruit and all the nuts a little at a time, mixing well.
16. Scrape down the sides of the bowl and the paddle.

Cake Directions:

1. Preheat the oven to 350 degrees F.
2. Lightly grease twelve 1-pound loaf pans.
3. Spoon about 1 cup of the batter into each pan.
4. Bake until golden and the tops spring back when touched, about 45 minutes (rearranging them after 25 minutes if necessary to brown evenly).
5. Cool for 10 minutes in the pans.
6. Remove cakes from the pans and cool completely on wire racks.
7. Combine the remaining 1/2 cup Grand Marnier and the bourbon. Without removing the cheesecloth, make tiny holes with a toothpick randomly on the top of each cake.
8. Brush the cakes with 1 cup of the reserved simple syrup.
9. Wrap each cake in a layer of cheese cloth. Set the cakes in a container and drizzle 1 tsp. of the bourbon mixture over each cake and set aside covered for three weeks. Drizzle 1 tsp. of the bourbon mixture over each of the cakes once every 3 to 4 days.
10. After three weeks, the cakes can be eaten or wrapped in plastic and stored in the refrigerator for up to 3 months, adding more liquor every couple of weeks.

Jam Fruitcake

Ingredients:

1 cup butter
2 cups white sugar
3 eggs
1 tsp. baking soda
3 cups all-purpose flour
1 cup buttermilk
1 cup blackberry preserves
1 cup chopped pecans
1 cup shredded coconut
1 cup raisins

Directions:

1. Preheat oven to 350 degrees F (175 degrees C).
2. Lightly grease one 10 inch tube pan and set aside.
3. Cream together the butter and sugar.
4. Add eggs separately, beating well after each.
5. Sift together soda and flour.
6. Add alternately with buttermilk to creamed mixture.
7. Mix well.
8. Add jam, pecans, coconut and raisins.
9. Mix well and pour into prepared pan.
10. Bake for one hour or until toothpick inserted in center comes out clean.

About the Author

Laura Sommers is **The Recipe Lady!**

She is a loving wife and mother who lives on a small farm in Baltimore County, Maryland and has a passion for all things domestic especially when it comes to saving money. She has a profitable eBay business and is a couponing addict. Follow her tips and tricks to learn how to make delicious meals on a budget, save money or to learn the latest life hack!

Visit her Amazon Author Page to see her latest books:

amazon.com/author/laurasommers

Visit the Recipe Lady's blog for even more great recipes and to learn which books are **FREE** for download each week:

http://the-recipe-lady.blogspot.com/

Subscribe to The Recipe Lady blog through Amazon and have recipes and updates sent directly to your Kindle:

The Recipe Lady Blog through Amazon

Laura Sommers is also an Extreme Couponer and Penny Hauler! If you would like to find out how to get things for **FREE** with coupons or how to get things for only a **PENNY**, then visit her couponing blog **Penny Items and Freebies**

http://penny-items-and-freebies.blogspot.com/

Other Books by Laura Sommers

- **Christmas Stuffing Recipes**
- **Christmas Hot Chocolate Recipes**
- **Christmas Cookies**
- **Candy Corn Cookbook**
- **Halloween Recipes**
- **50 Pumpkin Recipes**
- **Recipes for Leftover Thanksgiving or Christmas Turkey**

May all of your meals be a banquet
with good friends and good food.

Printed in Poland
by Amazon Fulfillment
Poland Sp. z o.o., Wrocław